Copyright © 2024 GLH Genevieve L. Hughes

Contents

WHAT WOULD YOU SACRIFICE TO REACH THE TOP?

Bound & Disarray

GLH
GENEVIEVE L. HUGHES

REPRIEVE BOOK 3

This book was written old school, with pen and paper, by a human writer.

No AI was used in the writing process in any form.
National Library of Australia pre-publication reference: NLApp110727.

Ebook ASIN: B0D6D9JM2Y
Paperback: 9798327807594

A catalogue record for this book is available from the National Library of Australia

This ebook may not be resold or shared.
Copyright: GLH, Genevieve L. Hughes
Original cover art, headers and photos: GLH
Fonts: Georgia and Carlsons Script.
Cover typography licensed by Canva.

Content Warning

If you are personally traumatized or triggered by reading material, perhaps this novel isn't for you.

This is a light-hearted work of fiction, with 18+ adult situations depicted.

Fictional liberties were taken, in the writing of this novel.

This novel contains coarse and sexually explicit language, and imagery.

Mention of:
Divorce.
Death due to foul play.
Loss of a partner.

Kaye is a curvy female lead, while Noel is a young, cinnamon roll character.

Dedication

Hey little petal in my stories. I see you. Don't worry, I blocked the other accounts who stalk, so good job.

Enjoy!

∞ ∞ ∞

$\mathcal{Synopsis}$

Noel

Broken flowers are my specialty. I'm able to envision the beauty they hide, and encourage them to thrive and bloom.

This one's a keeper. Such a shame she doesn't understand her value outside of the boardroom.

Kaye

My work has been my life for as long as I can remember.

I can't believe how quickly time passed me by. What do I have to offer a soul as old as Noel's with a mouth as dirty as a sailor's.

I don't understand what he sees in me, but the heat in the bedroom sets fire to the furnishings. Sometimes love finds you at the most inopportune moments.

Prologue

Kaye

Dream Date Night Auction, Baycrest Yacht Club

Robert escorts me to the temporary runway and podium. I drop my gavel and device, and raise a glass of bubbly to the room as he waits for the noise to settle. His introduction and welcome is brief, then with a nod, he departs, and leaves me to assess the audience.

I note a few staff are strategically placed to assist bidders. The floor gets a little heated at these events, and their assistance is vital in running a hassle free fundraiser.

A sea of faces look back at me, draped in fine couture, they're not getting any younger. These are the people I grew up with, my fellow cotillion members when we were presented to society; college alumni and friends, and should adore these moments. Instead, they feel stifled.

My dress this evening exposes my shoulders and the rosy burn of too much sun tints my pale complexion. I've never felt as if I fitted into this part of my life, an ugly duckling, not the elegant swan they wanted. No doubt Mother's going to comment about the new freckles gracing my complexion. She's never understood my love of vitamin D and fresh air. It's her loss. The few matronly frowns as I wandered through tonight told the same story. The same tired stories, and judgments, I've heard all my life from a crowd stuck in the past.

With a sigh, I pull back my burned shoulders and begin. "Good evening everyone. Welcome to our annual Dream Date Night. I'm Kaye, your auctioneer for tonight's festivities."

I teeter on insanely fragile heels and plaster a smile on my carmine-painted lips. I'm dressed the part, even if I don't feel it. "Terms are simple. Each bachelor's bio suggests their idea of the perfect date. Browse through the catalog. I'm sure there's something available for even the most discerning palate."

Already sloshed, the purple rinse crowd cheer—flushed faces and slightly glazed eyes prepare for battle. They're always guaranteed to provide a decent round of competitive bidding. While they may hang on tightly to their purse strings, their accounts are well-padded.

I spot Ms. Marx with her niece Tina, front and center, chomping at the proverbial bit, and I nod.

"I hope everyone's pockets are deep for our wonderful causes tonight. For those feeling generous, bids over a certain value may be deemed a charitable contribution deduction. Something to consider as you raise those batons and bring your checkbooks out."

And off we go.

Twenty-two able-bodied men later, from all walks of life, my favorite strides down the runway. Spurs ring on the stage floor, and the camel-colored chaps highlight his thick thighs. Dale shoots daggers, and his scowl departs with a whisper as I remind him it's for a worthy cause.

My brother doesn't know what's good for him, and this has to be the easiest way to fast-track his love life.

Without preamble, I offer my twin up as fresh meat to a group of scavengers. His sedate offer of a date—home cooking, a movie, and an early night—appears to excite a few.

Bidding paddles flash, as fast and sharp as shark's teeth. Hands snap, and numbers waive in my vision, but there can be only one winner.

Fierce and hungry for an unexpected prize, the winning patron—a stunning Asian-American beauty—appears as embarrassed, if not more so than my brother. Poor Belle hasn't had it easy of late, and Dale may be perfect for her.

"I believe the lovely Ms. Locke was the highest bidder. Congratulations, you'll not regret your win, I can assure you."

Ms. Marx mutters under her breath in the front, "Such a waste. She won't know what to do with so much man."

Words pour from my lips, though I contain myself and the volume. "What a bitch. Well Madame, if she doesn't, I'm sure my brother knows how to treat a lady."

Beady eyes squint through ghastly green-toned lids. "I missed the first part. Could you repeat yourself, dear?"

I slap my hand over my mouth, and feign a cough, "I said he's a great catch," and resume my job, as if nothing untoward was uttered.

"Please enjoy the dessert course doing the rounds with your coffee and liqueurs. This concludes our auction event for tonight. Thank you one and all for your support. Winning bidders, please settle your account with Mr. Preston and collect your terms of engagement for your dates."

Chapter One

Noel

With Robert indisposed, I've been designated our lady auctioneer's assistant as she confirms her hand written transactions are accurately transposed. "Preston sent me to collect you, Mrs. Reid. I'm Noel."

Sparkling blue eyes take me in. Her straight, bourbon-colored hair conflicts with a pale complexion. "Kaye. Please don't call me Mrs. Reid. I may be getting there, but I'm not ready to be my mother quite yet."

"Apologies, Ma'am."

"And that'll be a no to the ma'am too, thank you very much. Just Kaye is fine."

"Well, Just Kaye, Preston awaits your company in the office." I offer my arm, as she rocks unsteadily. "New shoes, Kaye?"

Exasperated, she balances against me and pops each one off. "Shh, no one needs to know," her conspiratorial grin is almost my undoing.

We both stare at her bare feet which contradict the elegant ensemble draping her curves. Her big toe is bruised, and the nail appears black and painful. "Your secret's safe with me, Kaye. One thing though, do you have an aversion to shoes?"

"I have a dislike of anything restrictive and expected of me. Shoes included."

"And your toe? No shoes on at the time?" I chuckle inwardly, her lips purse, and I wait for a scalding.

"A slight altercation with a potted plant this morning."

"Please tell me it survived your surprise attack." I take a quick sniff of her hair escaping from her coiffed locks, and push the stray strand behind her ear. "Child of the earth? Hmm, I like that."

Her harsh intake of breath, and swipe of her tongue over suddenly dry lips, sends an unexpected pulse to my cock.

"It's a little worse for wear. It could have been worse." Visibly shaking the thought from her mind, Kaye's all business again. "Show me the way then, Noel. Let's confirm those accounts, get them signed off, and we can relax for the evening."

Thirty minutes, and a few handsy patrons later, Kaye's done.

"So handsome, what brings you to tonight's auction?" her

breathy voice tempts.

"I'm the plant hire guy, if you must know."

I'm proud of the little business I've grown. There's no shame in what I do. My family views it as a temporary thing, but I've built a strong reputation and foundation in the local area.

"I wondered where they found the living props for this evening. The citrus trees were a lovely touch, you have a great sense of style." She eyes my lack of clothing and corny pink bow tie. "Tell me, how did you end up with the wait staff then?"

"A favor for a favor. My buddy Steve runs a temp business on the side. He was short-staffed tonight, so I picked up the work and watched my kids at the same time."

"Do you need to stay back, to I guess, pack up or…"

"No. Not tonight. Steve will come back tomorrow with a few of the guys, and gently take my babies home."

She slides fingertips across my chest, her nails enticing me to lean in closer, and whispers, "Did you have something else in mind for me to do?"

There's a hint of alcohol on her breath and I try to assess her sobriety. "Wouldn't want to do anything you'll regret in the morning now, Kaye."

"Let me fill you in on something, Noel. I live life without regret. It's too short, and whatever else they say." She shrugs her sun-kissed shoulders absently disregarding my attempt at chivalry. "I have a car waiting, if you're interested?"

∞ ∞ ∞

Kaye

Clasping Noel's hand, I lead the way through the dispersing crowd, to the coat check.

Goosebumps are followed by a shiver up the arm of the bronzed god beside me.

"How rude of me. Do you have a change of clothes or something to collect?"

His mouth lifts in a cheeky grin, "Give me a few, I'll be back." I watch form-fitting pants hug his tight ass, as he returns to the locker rooms, and I lose myself in his beauty.

"Your ticket ma'am?" I'm pulled from my trance, reminded of my coat, and hand the scrunched slip of paper over.

"Thank you," still distracted by my lack of etiquette, I look for a tip jar and remember it's not appropriate at the Club. "Have a wonderful evening, Mason."

Passersby stop and chat. I notice my brother, as he attempts to sneak out. "Dale. You can't avoid me forever. Don't forget to thank me for your stunning prize."

"I'm not sure if I need to thank you, or to curse you tonight, Sis."

"It could have been worse, Ms. Marx was right there until the last minute."

Dale's chuff reminds me he does have a sense of humor tucked away somewhere still. "I think I'd have placed a bid myself if Eveline Marx stood a chance of winning me."

"She had a message for you, by the way. Ms. Marx didn't think Belle would know what to do with you. Make sure you take care of her. Treat her well, Dale."

"I've never not been gentle with a woman. I'll be sure to show her a great time, wrap her up, and send her home to bed alone."

"Not what I meant…"

"Thanks for the advice, Sis. And the date too. Do you need a lift?"

"I'm fine, I have a car waiting." Noel slides in beside me, pressed pants and blazer highlighting his artfully arranged look. "Have you met Noel?"

Dale's brows rise, and a smug look is soon replaced by a welcoming hand. "I don't believe I have."

"Noel, this is my brother Dale."

"The Cowboy," he grabs Dale's hand in a strong grip. "Loved the nod to the silver screen. Great costume."

"A worthy cause and all that. I can't claim credit, it was all on Kaye." I watch Dale size up Noel as they come to some sort of silent agreement. "Well, I'm heading home. Thanks for setting me up Kaye. Enjoy the rest of your evening."

With Dale's departure, the silence between us becomes awkward. "Your place then?" I'm not inclined to take him home, a fling is one thing, but those pertinent details and the morning after are another.

"I'm a little way out of town, so what about a motel? We have several options close by."

"I'll let you choose." The four-door awaits with my driver.

Noel scrolls his phone, pulling up a booking app. This feels too much like a seventies hookup flick.

He nods to the driver, "Brampton Arms, on Gage Street, please."

Kaye

No time is wasted checking in, getting hot and heavy in the elevator. Skirt hiked up, his fingers dive in and out, thumb pressed against my clit. "Fuck you're so wet, baby."

Locking lips, he increases the tempo, I scream my orgasm into his mouth and wilt, boneless against him.

"I need inside you, so fucking bad." Hands continue to wander over my body, supporting me as I come back down to earth.

Hitting the door button, I'm half carried, half dragged into the sparse room. Dropped unceremoniously on the firm, austerely made bed, I watch the show as he divests himself of shirt and blazer, and crawls cat-like toward me.

A sculpted torso hovers over me, legs brace either side of my hips. *Look, don't touch*, runs in deep sapphire ink across his left pec and wraps through a glyph. Peering closer, no, it's a rune. "Where do I know this symbol from?"

Noel groans, his cock rubs encased in black silk, against my thigh and sends a current of heat through my lower body. "Something I was into as a teenager. It's not important right now."

I trace the lines, as he dry humps my leg. "Are you always this horny?"

"Kaye."

"Yes, Noel?"

"Get under the covers, so I can fuck you through the mattress."

Uncontrolled laughter sets me off. "Was that supposed to be a turn-on?"

He flashes pearly whites, "Yeah. It usually works."

"Me, Noel, big alpha male. You Kaye, get in bed, or else." I'm overcome with the plethora of cheesy phrases I'm spouting. "That's what you expect? What about suck my cock?"

He groans in pleasure, "I'll take that, sure."

"Pass. What else do you have in your corny repertoire?" Giggling would be cliche, so I bite back the need to laugh.

"All the girls love it. It's part of my charm."

"And there we have it. The girls love it. I haven't been a girl in a lifetime, Noel. My taste matured with my age." My mood crashes, disappointed by our conversation. I grab my clothes and hurriedly dress.

"Hey, don't go. We were starting to have fun weren't we, Kaye?"

"We were, Noel, but the buzz-kill is the generational difference. I'm not a kid anymore."

"It's what, six years, Dale said? Only a pinch of time between us. Stop fixating on the numbers."

"Dale? My *brother* Dale? Now this makes so much more sense. Look, this was fun, thank you. I'll let myself out, ok."

"Kaye, wait."

I can hear Noel swearing at his clothes, as I'm almost to the door.

"At least give me your number, Kaye. We had fun, and not because of Dale's interference."

"Bye, Noel. Thanks for the orgasm." I hear the door latch behind me, and pull up the app for a car, exiting the motel.

Waiting on the curb, the constant drizzle adds to my mood. The rain's going to ruin my coat, I'm dubious the dry cleaner will be able to salvage it.

"I can't believe this is my life."

"You and me lady," the driver mutters from the sleek black four-door in front of me. "Reid? You booked a car uptown?"

"Sure did."

Chapter Two

Kaye - Nine months later

"**T**hank you for today." Dale sweeps me into his arms, and onto the dance floor.

Despite the drama of his new bride's projectile vomiting mid service, I don't remember seeing my brother this happy in forever.

"It was my pleasure. I'm excited for both of you, and now…"

"We're about to become three. I know, hell, the boys have already ribbed me over this one."

"You'll make things work because you love her. Honestly, it's perfect."

The music ceases, and I'm reminded of the auction evening, with similar decorations lining the venue. "May I have this dance?" A voice like aged whiskey slides against my ear, and Dale hands me over to my next partner.

"Glad you could make it, Noel. Look after her."

Caught up in the rhythm of the next piece, I don't have time to argue. Warm hands glide along my bare back, and I'm pulled in close. "You smell amazing."

I shiver at his proximity, and relax into something I know won't end well. "So do you. Did you hide out until I couldn't escape this time?"

"No, sorry to disappoint you. I was running late, mechanical issues with my truck. Plant guy, remember."

Champagne emboldens me, as our connection sparks again. "Well, as you've arrived at the party last minute, we could always take this somewhere else, once the bride and groom have left, of course."

"A woman who knows exactly what she wants. Hmm, and where do you suggest we relocate our celebration?'

"I'm sure you promised to show me the wonders of your, what was it?"

"My blossoms? Maybe the potting benches and the warmth of the orchid hothouse?"

I edge in closer, and allow the moment to envelop me. What could possibly go wrong, with a quick fling?

"I forgive you, in case you wanted to know. Dale meant well, setting us up last time."

"Thank you. I think they're leaving."

I realize the music has stopped, and we're standing in the midst of the event winding down. "Perfect timing. Let's get out of here."

Chapter Three

Noel

Raindrops slip from the magnolia petals like tiny dancers, elusive in the rising heat.

The smell of geosmin, as the soil wakes, wafts to me, comforting in its familiarity. I pick a full-bodied bloom, handling her gently—a reminder of the woman in my bed.

I wander into the first hothouse checking humidity and temperature, then update the digital log. The Kentias need repotting soon, their roots protrude from their pots, begging for the soil below to embrace them. Racks of the next generation of seedlings look promising, as do the Hare's Foot and Boston ferns in hanging planters. I leave notes for Tony to spray the citrus on return, and rotate the stock ready for our next event.

Locking the door between the greenhouses, I'm excited to check the tissue cultures in the orchid room. The lights are already on, highlighting the sea of plants in various stages of growth.

Phalaenopsis in deep burgundy hues are surrounded by a sea of cream. A wedding favorite, and staple in my business. Soft pinks and mottled yellow, bright clear whites; a range of colors for every occasion from weddings to funerals.

The cultures have a second leaf peeping out in most of the agar trays. A new hybrid clone, as we experiment with prolific growers and larger flower spikes.

My favorite time of day is before the world rises, and the noise of residential development begins. My safe haven, may not be so for much longer.

The threat of development and inevitable relocation hang heavy on my shoulders.

Back at the house, I find Kaye wrapped in my favorite sweatshirt, a coffee in hand.

"Did you sleep well?"

I watch her uncurl, face relaxed, free of makeup and pretense. "Like a log, thanks to our extracurricular activities."

"I've done my rounds, how about breakfast?"

She awkwardly waves her cup, "Found mine thanks. Your rounds?"

"I'm the plant guy, remember? Well it entails getting dirty, managing greenhouses, and you know, plants."

"You'll have to show me some time. Right now, however, I need to get going. As much as I'd love to stay."

"It's a Saturday. You don't get a day off to unwind?"

"I did this morning." She points to her empty cup. "This is a lazy morning for me, but no day off. Not in the cutthroat world I work. There's always a drama, a prima donna whose work isn't edited, ready in time. Any slew of fires to put out."

"Ashes to ashes, crematorium dust kind of dramas?"

"We're always playing with fire, so yeah."

Chapter Four

Kaye

I woke to an empty bed, the pillow beside me cold. Light filtered through the open windows, and the sound of rain tempted me outside.

A discarded sweatshirt, and a quick shower; I grab a hot coffee from the waiting pot. The silence is calming, and a balm to my soul.

Noel comes into my periphery and I watch his unguarded return to the house through the bedroom window. Tousled hair, brushed back from his face, highlights harsh planes and an aquiline nose. Those lips I remember oh so vividly as he went down on me last night.

Shirt sleeves rolled up, he pauses, and tilts his head to the drizzle. A look of pure bliss crosses his features. He's a beautiful specimen. It's such a pity he's so much younger than me.

He greets me, and I make my excuses to head back to the city. The temptation to stay and play hooky is overridden by my need to protect myself.

The drive back is uneventful on deserted, lazy Saturday roads. I pull into the undercover car park, grab a change of clothes from the rear seat, and head into work, pondering how this is the sum total of life. I watched my twin marry his second chance at love yesterday, briefly attended the wedding reception, got laid by my idea of a perfect man, and now I'm back in the office.

Nostalgia kicks in with all those things I could have been. How many times did I trade my happiness for my job? Having passed the big four-o, I see my mid-life crisis looming. I'm thankful for small mercies, and my twin's newfound happiness. Belle made a beautiful bride. When she picked Dale up as an auction win, his life turned around. No longer sulking about his big old empty house, Belle's brought light into his dark world.

Did I pick up a Millennial from a bathroom mishap? Sure. Baby blues, and a lightly dusted v, tracked all the way down to heaven. I still see his angelic face every time I come. Noel's one night of bliss has filled my spank bank for years to come, and he's topped it up again. I kind of wish he'd grace my bed, the same way he filled me last night, and every one after. But what the hell am I thinking? I'm not girlfriend material. I'm a workaholic, with a noose around my neck and family commitments.

Dale's youngest is marrying his best friend, and his new wife pregnant, and due who knows when. I don't have time to explain our generational differences, but hell, Noel pushed all the right buttons.

"Good morning, Ms. Reid," Janet's perky morning greeting echoes from her connecting office. "Is there anything you need?"

"Provided the coffee is strong, I'm fine thanks, Janet. How was your Friday evening?"

Her eyes light up as she recounts her night out. A new band, an eatery, and an early night. "It was the perfect end to the week. Thanks for asking. And you, Ms. Reid? Did you have a pleasant time at the reception?"

"It was different, in a good way, Janet." I cut off her aim to draw me out on more personal topics. "Messages? Anything I need to dive straight into, or did the world survive my afternoon off?"

"Messages on your desk. There's a note from your sister-in-law regarding a contract. A few queries on a cover graphic an author dislikes."

"Thanks, Janet. I'll deal with Kat on Monday. I don't want my weekend ruined." With no love lost between my brother's ex-wife and myself, I'm happy to leave her on the back burner to stew for a few days. "Whose cover?"

"The cartoon one for Lori Jayden. The art department provided faceless mock-ups, the author's taken offense."

"I'm not surprised. We're not ashamed of content here, I warned she wouldn't appreciate them, regardless of trends."

"I'll quote Lori," Janet deepens her voice and twirls her hair. "If I wanted to write closed fucking door, I'd set fire to the words before I wrapped them in that generic crud."

"She was that impressed. Hand them back to the art department and tell them to spice things up. If there are no other pressing issues, I'll be unavailable while I look through things."

"I'll have your coffee ready in a few minutes then." She pauses, and I feel the avalanche heading my way. "I printed this off, but you may want to check the blog posts, sorry."

Great, just what I need.

WE'RE BACK KIDDIES. NEWLY RELEASED JOURNALS
FROM MURDERED BLOGGER, COME WRITER, EVIE
CAMPBELL, HAVE SURFACED. YES, THEY'VE BEEN
AUTHENTICATED. IT WAS ONLY A MATTER OF TIME
BEFORE HER TRUTH SAW THE LIGHT.

I don't need a reality check, but load the website we all avoid, and open up my chat with Jade. I pray for clarity from someone with sense this morning.

Jade

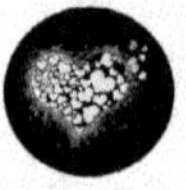

Kaye   **Jade**

Jade, You'll never guess who I bumped into at Dale's wedding.

Your mystery man?

I'm that predictable?

No, but it's been how many months since a random one-night stand and you're still mooning over him?

I'm not mooning. He's become my vibrator's bestie.

Too much information thank you!

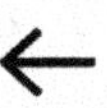

Kaye

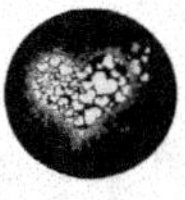

Jade

The mental image of ocean blue eyes gets me off in minutes, every single time. It's not my time though, this infatuation is crazy.

Since when is it not your turn?

I passed the big four-zero, and then some. I work a sixty-hour week, if it's a slow one, and split my routine between swimming and running.

Why not let your blond god make a decision on what time it is then?

Maybe. Look, I have to get back to work. The crap piled up today doesn't look promising. I'll check in later.

Have fun not doing anything I wouldn't do!

Enter your message...

Looking back to my laptop, the page has loaded and the offending blog is active once more. It had been silent since Evie's untimely death. What did they have to gain after all of this time?

∞ ∞ ∞

The Jolly Roger Blog post

A link blinks at the bottom of the page. What can it hurt?

∞ ∞ ∞

One, two, three, four, someone scanned my playbook's wall.
Silly goose, didn't they work out how far back this went?

Five, six, seven, eight, now it's time for the final date.
Hmm, I'm sorry I'll not be there to watch this
go down. Did they believe nobody noticed?

Playtime is over. It's time to pay Charon his due.

Lots of love,

Evie xox

Chapter Five

Kat

We buried Evie in December. Christmas will never be the same again.

Those boxes I mentioned moving, protecting—wait until you read what they contained. What was worth taking a life for? Names. Dates. Places. But, I'm getting ahead of myself. My name is Kat, and I'm hijacking Kaye's happily ever after.

When is the most important time of the year for a reader? Post Christmas sales, armed with a gift card or certificate. The promise of new discoveries, or old favorites, burns a hole in pockets.

Evie planned her windfall, right down to the delivery of her little pink book to the biggest legitimate news source, aka gossip blog. And so it began.

The Jolly Roger Blog post

CONSIDER THIS IDEA. ROMANCE IS A DIRTY WORD.

PROMISCUITY IS FORBIDDEN.
SELF GRATIFICATION: IMMORAL.

HEAVEN HELP A WOMAN WHO THINKS FOR THEMSELF.

NOW, MAKE THIS PLOT INTO A ROMANCE NOVEL. A BEST
SELLER. SOLD TO WOMEN, BY MEN, WHO HATE WOMEN.

IS IT THE GREATEST CRIME, OR THE MOST SUCCESSFUL
CON OF ALL TIME? THE MOST INGENIOUS SCAM,
PERHAPS.

DID YOU FALL FOR IT TOO?

My message app buzzes, and a name I didn't expect to see appears.

If she's going to rip me a new one for not going into the chapel yesterday, I'll be happy to educate her on being a responsible adult.

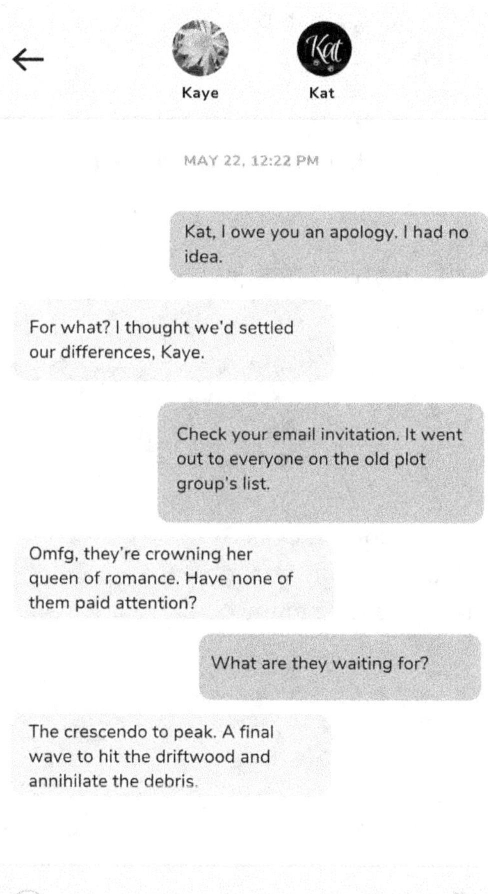

Kaye **Kat**

Won't that cloud the waters further?

Think grander. A final cleanse, followed by a pure, clean platform. Artists, writers and truths.

Do you believe it will happen?

No, too many are blind to their true nature.

So why bother? If they've won, what's your endgame?

To be honest, I don't fucking know. All I know is this has left a bitter taste and a hole in my heart.

  Kaye  Kat

> Don't go there, Kat. Evie wouldn't want this.

Evie didn't want to die by their hand either, Kaye. Someone has to accept responsibility for her death.

> What if I told you someone attempted to?

Tell me you didn't open up communications with them?

> I'll send you a picture. Please don't be mad at me.

THE MINISTRY OF ROMANCE FORMALLY REQUESTS YOUR ATTENDANCE, IN CELEBRATION OF ARIAN KHALINE. OUR INTERVIEW WITH KASAMINE IS NOT ONE TO BE MISSED.

DAUGHTER OF A, LETS SAY A HIGHLY INFLUENTIAL CRIME LORD, AND DISGRACED EUROPEAN PRINCESS; ARIAN ROSE FROM A LIFE OF CRIME, TO THE HALLOWED HALLS OF BEST-SELLING ROMANCE.

ARIAN'S BOOKS ARE EXQUISITE WORKS OF ART, WORTHY OF ANY TROPHY SHELF.

WE LOOK FORWARD TO YOUR RSVP, NO LATER THAN JUNE 1ST.

Kaye

Kat

...what the ever loving fuck. Kaye, this is an admission of guilt.

An anonymous admission, something we can't act on. Leave it with me.

Chapter Six

Press release

J.D. Publishing's latest from deceased in-house author, Evie Campbell, promises to tear down the barriers between hacks and writers.

The chasm between legitimate talent and recycled plastics grows deeper with each new 'product' added to vanity house rosters.

Sources once close to the reclusive author believe her tell all manifesto is about to go big or go home—live streamed and unfiltered.

Between rave reviews and did not finish ratings—with no middle ground—this author had nothing to lose. As she's been quoted before, *'someone with nothing to lose is dangerous.'*

I guess it's up to the reading audience now to make

comparisons between theirs and Evie's experiences. We only hope you survive the aftershocks.

The Jolly Roger Blog post

THE JOLLY ROGER BLOG

WE'RE BACK KIDDIES. NEWLY RELEASED JOURNALS FROM MURDERED BLOGGER, COME WRITER, EVIE CAMPBELL, HAVE SURFACED. YES, THEY'VE BEEN AUTHENTICATED. IT WAS ONLY A MATTER OF TIME BEFORE HER TRUTH SAW THE LIGHT.

THE JOLLY ROGER BLOG

INTERVIEW: WELCOME TO ROMANCELANDIA.

EVIE CAMPBELL AUGUST 2022 - JOURNAL ENTRY.

IN 2015 I NAIVELY STEPPED INTO THE DRAMA OF INDIE TEAMS. THE PUSH TO PROMOTE CHEAP, REPLICATED, DUMBED DOWN WORDS, AT ANY COST.

TODAY, SEVEN YEARS LATER, THOSE SAME BLOGGERS RULE OVER THE INDUSTRY WE LOVE. HOW, YOU MIGHT ASK? BY ANY MEANS NECESSARY. THEY BECAME THE AUTHORS WITH AN INSTANT FOLLOWING AS BENEVOLENT READERS.

NOTHING IS SACRED. NO ONE IS PROTECTED. EVERYONE IS SUSPECT. THIS IS MY FINAL INTERVIEW.

THE JOLLY ROGER BLOG

WITH THE PREVALENCE OF WRITING SOFTWARE—THE FRONT END TO ARTIFICIAL INTELLIGENCE'S SCRAPING OF DATA—PERHAPS SOME ARE IGNORANT. THEY'RE FEW AND FAR BETWEEN. RESEARCH IS PARAMOUNT WHEN WRITING. IN THEIR CASE, IT MAY BE BLISSFUL NOT TO COMPREHEND THEIR CRIME, AFTER ALL, THEY FAIL TO RESEARCH OUTSIDE OF A TV SHOW. BUT A CRIME EXISTS.

HOW DID SO MANY NEW NAMES ARISE, OR REINVENT, DURING A WORLDWIDE PANDEMIC? SIMPLE. TOO MANY CLOSED THEIR EYES. THEY TOOK WHAT WASN'T THEIRS, AND THEY'LL NEVER APOLOGIZE. WHAT'S THE GOLDEN RING WORTH? HOW MANY SOLD THEIR SOULS?

THE JOLLY ROGER BLOG

THING IS IT WON'T CHANGE. IT'S ONLY GOING TO GET WORSE. WHEN SOMEONE GAMBLES THEY WON'T BE CAUGHT, AND BELIEVES THEY'RE TOO BIG TO BE HELD ACCOUNTABLE, THEY'VE ALREADY WON.

HAVING ERODED AWAY THE CONFIDENCE OF LEGITIMATE TALENT, BETWEEN ONE STAR REVIEWS, AND WITNESSING THEIR OWN WORDS BECOME BEST SELLERS—WHY WOULD ANYONE WITH A HINT OF SANITY FIGHT BACK?

IF YOU READ, WRITE AND REVIEW, ASK YOURSELF, ARE YOU COMPLICIT IN THEIR CRIMES?

DO YOU FEEL TAINTED? GUILTY? OR DO YOU HONESTLY BELIEVE THEY'RE ABOVE REPROACH, WORTH SAVING?

Chapter Seven

Kaye

Four weeks later

"There's a delivery here for you Ms. Reid," Janet's perky tone is filled with excitement.

"Put it wherever, Janet. And thank you."

"I'm not sure it's that simple."

I look up from my computer to a flourish of orange and cream blossoms, splashed between green. The scent of citrus fills the office. I grin to myself. The memory invokes a night of passion I'll never forget.

"Aren't they beautiful?" She snaps a leaf, the smell of fresh imperials floods the room.

"There are orchids also. Where would you like them left?"

I glance at the face behind the sea of greenery, blond hair peaks from a backward cap. "If they're not to your liking, I'm sure the vendor will accept them back."

"That will be all, Janet, thank you. Could you bring coffee for me and my guest please."

A conspiratorial grin lights her face and she spins to do my bidding.

"You can tell the vendor I'm grateful for the delivery. I may need them redirected to my home address however."

"I'm sure that can be arranged."

"Thank you Noel. You don't know how much this means today."

"I've watched the tabloids. It's been hard to miss your face and the family business plastered everywhere lately."

"Thank you. I love you remembered I enjoyed the orange trees. But this is too much."

"For you, no it's not. How about I drop them to your place? They come with an invitation, by the way. A hearty meal and weekend at the nursery. A redo of our first date."

"We didn't date, Noel. We screwed ourselves silly."

"Well I like silly, and I think we're due for a repeat performance. My place, at eight. Bring whatever you're working on, and a packed bag. You need a hideaway for a few days, and I'm offering."

"I can't drop everything, we have deadlines. Are you sure it's ok to bring my work with me?"

"Small business owner, don't forget. Work is part of who we are. Load up whatever you need to handle, just be there by eight."

Chapter Eight

Kat

Journal entry

Someone vaguely posted about authors who felt privileged enough not to include trigger warnings. I'll refute their privileged—woke mindset is destroying our work.

If you feel you can do better, join the cult offering pages of warnings. I'll give you a hint, they rarely deliver on those promises. It's a marketing ploy.

There's chaos in creation.

Stealing a few sentences does not make a writer. A thief, sure.

Words are sustenance to the soul. A good book will feed the mind. A great yarn, well, that will feed your body.

Chapter Nine

Kaye

Reluctantly, I'd accepted the olive branch extended by Noel. It's strange to be back at the nursery. He'd cooked an amazing meal, filled the house, no, not a house– a home, with warmth. Despite his playboy persona, I think he's a homebody like me. His company and our blossoming relationship feels right.

Beside me, my work for the weekend lays ready, as I absently itch to open the pages of a carefully prepared manuscript. A life story, non fiction, representing the devious nature of the art of literature.

My thoughts are disturbed by blood red wine refilling my glass. It will only add to the flush of my skin, as the heat from the fire comforts me.

"What tickled your sense of humor? I don't think I've heard

you laugh like that before."

"Have you read this, Kaye?" Next to me again, Noel waves a pretty pink proof copy, he snagged from my work stack.

"Not yet. I threw in a little light reading, in case."

"You didn't think I'd keep you entertained? Shame on you." Another page flip of the novel finds it thrown on the sofa between us. "I can't, I'm sorry." Noel roars with laughter, as he holds his sides. "Please tell me it's not serious. You're not releasing a brand dropping replication of a decent piece of literature."

A quick glance at the title tells me the author is a best seller in the eighteen to twenty five-year-old age bracket. "I've not read this book yet, but reviewers claim her stories are well written."

"Hardly well written if there's a brand drop going on. Haven't they heard of trademark infringement?"

"You know how these younger writers are, they claim it's part of their art."

"Damn shame they can't string sentences together effectively."

"They'll all inform you, quite rudely I might add, they hold degrees."

"In what, typos and plagiarism?"

"It's a difficult situation. We simply contract those who've gone viral, the fans love the childlike style apparently and forgive errors for story quality."

"But the original source, by that I mean I've read this before, was beautifully constructed art." He rubs the rune on his chest and winks. "This knockoff reads like a fashion column, outlining a runway walk from her brand name shoes, to the ombré acrylic nails with added sparkle."

"Oh my god. You've hit the nail on the head. I vaguely remember picking up a synopsis for another book from last summer." I wrack my brain, but fail to remember the title. "It was written as if they were viewing a fashion show. While the clothes and jewelry were detailed, the rest was flat and bland."

"And this is one of your authors on the roster? Someone who's contributed to the decline in quality of everything in print?"

I shrug off the growing feeling something is amiss with our team. "Perhaps they majored in journalism in college?"

"Who knows. But they're not writers." He opens to a dog eared page. "Fine, black patent leather (insert brand) heels, the red soles are fit for any French fashion show. The sleek (insert brand) dress...' Need I say more?"

A text message arrives, my phone vibrates on the coffee table. "I need to check it. Hold that thought."

There's another blog update, great.

Chapter Ten

Jolly Roger Blog post

And so it begins...

THE JOLLY ROGER BLOG

AND WE'RE BACK! A TELL ALL FROM THE GRAVE IS BEING RELEASED PAGE BY PAGE, ON ONE OF THE LARGEST SOCIAL MEDIA PLATFORMS EVER. WE HAVE MORE EXCLUSIVE CONTENT TO TEASE YOUR SENSES.

I prepared the Romancelandia manifesto, as an experiment in market trends—until it wasn't. In the belief my time is limited, I've handed this to the only person who's brave enough to out them on my death.

How did the average rise to star spangled fame? They were borderline illiterate, stay at home moms, who lived vicariously through book porn. Who was the genius in this scam?

Someone orchestrated selling an author's writing back to readers, rinsed clean. With enough of the content and plot to remain within, to pull sales, it had to be recognized by conscientious devotees.

If queried, those responsible told you she was developing her own style. She was on a mission to find her place in a market. Always a means to justify theft, pure and simple—then they were silenced.

How the fuck does your style alter book to book? It doesn't. Maybe the mixing software chosen does. It's all via online apps. As one is shut down, connected to scams and plagiarism, another evolves.

How the hell do they find these programs? We all acknowledge those who can write. Those who can't purchase software subscriptions. They're evolving as we speak.

Greed driven, who decides to step out of a bubble and go looking for more? One who demands to be crowned Queen in their five year plan.

She watched her teammates wallow as they failed each release. All the while she sits on a rotten throne, waiting for a pedicure.

I've read the sour cream of the current crop. If egos matched talent, we'd not be having this discussion.

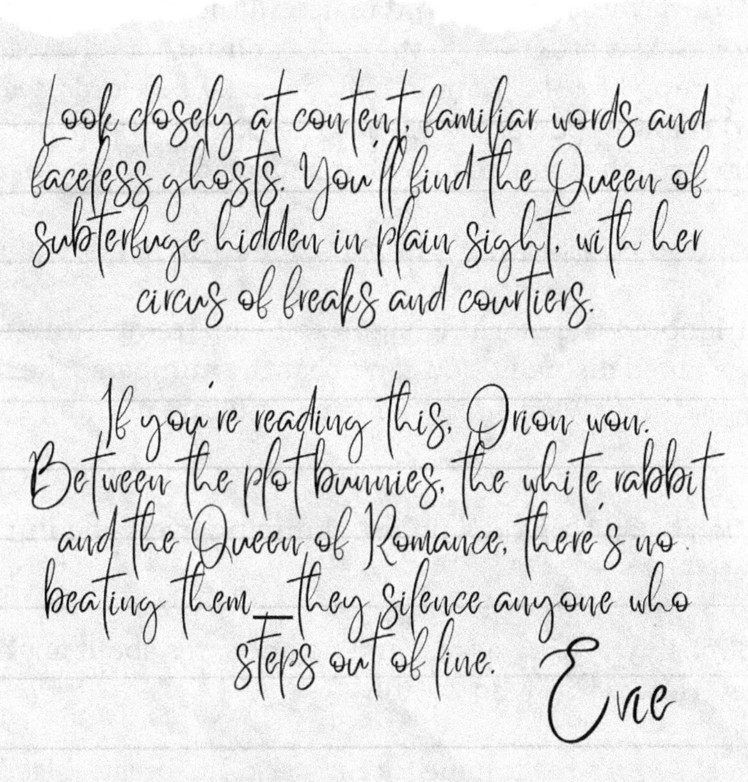

Noel leans over my shoulder, humming along with the background music. Right now, it's the only sound in the room.

"So, who killed Evie?" Noel leans in, and taps the word epilogue at the bottom of the post. "Are we going to turn the page and find out?"

"I don't need to. We all did."

His expression shifts to concern. "How can you believe that? You'd never hurt a fly."

"Evie devoured words and reviewed them like a machine. She knew she drew attention to the books and authors she read." I suck in a calming breath. "Damon held on to Evie's words, waiting for a marketable opportunity. He had the chance to save her, but saw dollar signs, choosing to make bank instead."

"And you? What was your part in this—in her downfall?"

"I ignored the warning signs as Evie attempted to shield us all. She failed dismally. You can't beat the numbers. The machine. Readers simply want a fix, an escape, and care nothing about who it hurts."

"Don't you think it's unfair, dumping everyone in the same basket?"

"Probably. A life was lost and no one cares about anything but money. How is this who we are?"

Noel swipes his tongue up my neck, his breath bleeding into my damaged soul. "You care. Kat cares. Those who've read this far care. Deep down;" He brushes my sternum, ghosting fingers over my breasts, peaking my nipples against the satin restraining my chest. "Deep down you knew this was inevitable, out of your control. Time to turn the last page."

Chapter Eleven

Kaye

Kaye   **Kat**

Kat, I know you said you're done, no more Romancelandia. How about we get serious and you write what you love?

There's no market for my work. I can't dumb it down to primary grade reading level to placate the masses.

What if I said change was afoot. Their little reign is over. Readers, publishers and outlets alike, are over the fake and fluffy.

I'd respond with pick a trope or genre, I'll play.

So, let's brainstorm. Do you want a shot at a trend? Pick a trope.

Enter your message...

Kaye

Kat

I'm in my rip off public domain era.

Ha, good one. No lol, I can go one better.

I doubt it pmsl.

Let's try remix your own ripped off work era.

You're killing me. What about song lyrics x small town x grumpy sunshine x sports x mafia x Wicca x best friend's sibling, and call it taboo?

You forgot to add diversity, fake ménage with a gay rep and you have a best seller.

Kaye

Kat

Pick a name. I love where this is going.

What about...

I know! Dynasty.

Brilliant, I think. As in, they're creating a new dynasty of crap?

You can only mix something so often, before it splits and floats to the surface.

Enter your message...

YOU READ IT HERE FIRST, KIDS. EVIE CAMPBELL'S
NOTES FROM THE AFTERLIFE. ENJOY!
ONCE UPON A TIME, A DEBUT AUTHOR USED A FAMILY
PEN NAME TO PUBLISH A LITTLE PARODY PIECE. WHILST
THEY HAD NOTHING TO HIDE, MAINTAINING DISTANCE
BETWEEN FICTION AND REALITY WAS THE SENSIBLE
THING TO DO.
SADLY FOR SAID PEN NAME, ON PUBLICATION THEY
DREW THE UNWANTED ATTENTION OF TROLLS ON A
REVIEW PLATFORM. HOW, WHO KNOWS, MILLIONS OF
BOOKS ARE PUBLISHED DAILY. SENSIBLY, NO MATTER
WHAT NAME WAS USED, THEY WERE GOING TO FIND THE
WORK. THE PROBLEMATIC REVIEWERS HAD BEEN PART
OF THE MACHINE FOR TOO LONG.

BEFORE THEY COULD ESTABLISH THEIR AUTHOR PAGE, THE BOOK CONTENT WAS EDITED, AND THE ACCOUNT VAULTED. DID IT CEASE THERE, WITH ONE LITTLE NOVELLA? NO. THE HARASSMENT CONTINUED, THE NOBODY AUTHOR HAD FOUND THEMSELVES A STALKER OR THREE—TO THIS DAY, AND NO DOUBT WILL DO SO IN PERPETUUM.

SIMPLY, THIS IS HOW IT WORKS. SHE SHOULD HAVE KNOWN BETTER.

SOUNDS STRANGER THAN FICTION, RIGHT? THE WHOLE STORY DOES. IT'S SAD TO SAY, WHILE FICTIONALIZED, IT'S THE TIP OF A MASSIVE, SUBMERGED SHIT PILE OF AN ICEBERG, CLOAKED IN CORRUPTION.

THE JOLLY ROGER BLOG

SHE WAS ASKED FROM DAY ONE, WHAT DO YOU WANT? WHAT'S THE END GAME? SIMPLE, TO OPEN READERS' EYES TO THE POSSIBILITY NOT EVERYTHING THEY READ IS REAL. NOT EVERYTHING THEY SEE IS LEGITIMATE. TRUST YOUR GUT, NOT THE FIVE DOLLAR HOOKERS, AS THEY'VE BEEN CALLED BEFORE, PUSHING THE LATEST TO BEST SELLER LEVEL. NOT THE POORLY CONSTRUCTED FAMILIAR PLOT, CHARACTERS OR EVEN SYNOPSIS. THOSE WORDS ARE MOST LIKELY, NOT THEIR OWN.

HOW MANY TIMES HAVE YOU CLICKED THAT REC, ONLY TO QUESTION YOUR BESTIE'S BOOK TOUR GROUP'S JUDGMENT?

THE JOLLY ROGER BLOG

IF IT SOUNDS TOO GOOD TO BE TRUE, IT MOST LIKELY
IS.

WHAT DO I WANT? I WANT YOU TO OPEN YOUR EYES,
PAY ATTENTION TO THE SMOKE SCREENS, AND SEEK
OUT THE SOURCE WORKS. GIVE CREDIT WHERE IT'S DUE.
NOT TO THE PLOT BUNNIES SELLING RIPPED WORKS, OR
THE HYPE GIRLS WHO CREATED THE PLASTICS, OR THE
ONES REWORKING PUBLIC DOMAIN—JUST BECAUSE
THEY CAN. I'LL GIVE YOU A HINT, THEY'RE ALSO
REWORKING OTHER PUBLISHED WORKS, YOU'VE SIMPLY
NOT PAID ATTENTION.

QUESTION THE BENEFITS YOU RECEIVE IN TURN FOR
PROMOTING BOOKS AND LEAVING A STOCK STANDARD,
GENERIC REVIEW FOR A PRODUCT YOU SUSPECT ISN'T
REAL.

WHAT DO I WANT? ACCOUNTABILITY, HONESTY, AND TRUE TALENT TO BE SEEN.
I KNOW HOW THIS WORKS, I'VE SAT ON BOTH SIDES OF THE FENCE NOW. I'VE HAD MY OWN WORDS STOLEN BY THOSE IMAGINARY FRIENDS IN MY FEED. THOSE WORDS WERE SACRIFICED FOR A REASON.

∞ ∞ ∞

Twenty-four hours later

THE JOLLY ROGER BLOG

FAITH, LIES AND ROMANCE.
IT'S NOTHING MORE THAN A MASQUERADE. A STAGE
SHOW FOR THE NAIVE AND GULLIBLE. FOR THOSE
SEEKING SPICE AND DANGER—SUSTENANCE—OUTSIDE
OF THEIR DAY TO DAY LIVES. SHARKS IN A TINY POOL,
UNABLE TO SEE THE BIGGER PICTURE, SACRIFICE THEIR
OWN CREATIONS—SPAWN.
WE ALL HAVE AN AGENDA. SOUNDS CONSPIRATORIAL
DOESN'T IT? DON'T ASK ME WHAT MINE WAS, I
HONESTLY DON'T KNOW.
I DO KNOW, THOSE CLOSEST TO US ATTEMPT TO
DIRECT US. CONNECTIONS WITH OTHERS ALTER OUR
BEHAVIOR AND PATH, TO GUIDE OR SUIT THEIR OWN
AGENDA, DAILY.

THE JOLLY ROGER BLOG

THOSE RELATIONSHIPS MAY BE LIFE CHANGING, OR
EVEN MORE IMPORTANTLY, A RESTRICTIVE,
NARCISSISTIC CONTROL OF A NARRATIVE.
NEVER LET THE PRETTY FACES AND SWEET WORDS BE
YOUR OWN PERSONAL EXPERIENCE OF LIFE WITHIN THIS
COMMUNITY. STEP OUTSIDE, BREATHE AND DISCOVER
TRUTHS FOR YOURSELF.
OR DON'T. BE A SHEEP, AND FOLLOW THE RULES AND
HIERARCHY DESIGNATED TO YOU.
THE GUARDIANS OF WORDS ARE NOTHING MORE THAN
GATEKEEPERS. THEIR AGENDA—TO SUCCEED AT ALL
COSTS, WHILE CENSORING THE CONTENT YOU READ.

THE JOLLY ROGER BLOG

ASK YOURSELF, AS A READER—HOW MANY TIMES HAVE YOU PICKED UP A BOOK, ONLY TO PUT IT ASIDE? DID YOU QUERY YOUR BESTIE'S SENSE OF HUMOR, AND CONFIRM THEIR RECOMMENDATION WASN'T A HOAX? ALL WHILE CONSIDERING THE DRIVEL IN FRONT OF YOU, DID YOU DOUBT YOUR FRIENDS OWN WORTH AND ABILITY TO COMPREHEND WHY THIS IS A BEST SELLER? THIS IS THE CONTROLLED NARRATIVE OF AN INFLUENCER—NOT A READER.

∞ ∞ ∞

Journal entry

Kat

There was no Evie. No Kat. No white bunny. They were all components of those who participated, meshed together from broken pieces. None of them were whole. None of them belonged. It's what made them useful, strategic weapons.

Romancelandia was a creation. A mirage. A bank for the unscrupulous who preyed on the unwary.

Those with a semblance of decency were led by their heartstrings. Tenacious filaments of morality strung taught—manipulated by hacks who had no compunction in doing so.

Close your book, open your eyes. Step outside and experience the real world.

None of this was real. It couldn't be. If there was any chance it was, the queens owe a generation of stolen words reparation. Hide this if you wish, it will still stand when your day is over.

We need a scorched earth to cleanse Romancelandia. Someone strong enough, brave enough, to fight all of our demons.

Is it you, the reader?

Evie

Kat

Indie is a rock pool in an ocean of lies.

I warned you to pick sides early on. I'll make sure I end up on the winner's.

They have long memories when it comes to petty drama.

Let me guess, short when it comes to the truth?

Something like that, sure. Moreover, they'll hold indiscretions over your head as bargaining tools.

Threats? Ha. I received them on day one.

Evie

Kat

You threatened the security of their status quo.

Maybe I scared them a tiny bit?

Nothing tiny about the fear factor. You threatened their new cushy livelihood.

They think borrowing a word or two, here and there, is of no consequence.

It reminds me as a child, being told to be seen and not heard.

And how did that work for you?

Evie

Kat

 Not well. Trusting adults, believing in their protection, was a fallacy, why do you think I put pen to paper?

You can't change the past. Acceptance of self, of value, look how far you've come.

Until I stupidly stepped into the colosseum of lies. Their fairytale reproductions.

Nothing is new, we've heard it stated how many times?

The words were new. They were real, raw, and personal.

Failure to question familiarity was built on this motto.

Enter your message...

Evie

Kat

Lives. Now I understand the write from experience references. They stole writers' lives.

Their truths were spoken and gifted to the world. Fragile pieces of souls, taken for granted.

And these bitches took what wasn't theirs, and claimed it as their own.

More. Fool. Them. This is their only reprieve.

Epilogue

Evie's final entry.

THE JOLLY ROGER BLOG

WHEN DO YOU DECIDE IF IT'S ALL GONE TOO FAR? CAN YOU STILL SEE THE DELINEATION BETWEEN WHAT'S RIGHT AND WRONG? BETWEEN BLACK AND WHITE; OR ARE THEY ALL SHADES OF GRAY? HOW FAR DO YOU NEED TO BE BACKED INTO THE PROVERBIAL CORNER BEFORE YOU SNAP, OR RUN?

WHAT IF I WROTE MY STORY, AND DUMBED IT DOWN? ANY SEMBLANCE OF THOSE INVOLVED—REMOVED—TO PROTECT THEIR ANONYMITY. NOT FANFICTION, INSPIRED BY, OR BASED ON HERO WORSHIP. DON'T WORRY, THOSE WHO WERE UNABLE TO PICK UP ON THE SUBTLETIES OF WORDS, DID BELIEVE IT WAS FANFIC–A SLAP IN THE FACE–AND POINTED AT THEIR OPPONENTS. THEY ARE THE GUILTY PARTIES, OF COURSE.

THE JOLLY ROGER BLOG

THERE WERE NEVER WHISPERS AND SUGGESTIONS. THERE WAS NO PUPPET MASTER DIRECTING, ENCOURAGING, OR GHOST WRITING MY WORDS. THIS WAS WRITTEN PURELY AND SIMPLY FOR MYSELF. CONSIDER THESE WERE ACTUAL DIARY ENTRIES, AND YEARS OF RESEARCH WITH A THOUSAND PLUS BOOKS READ. WOULD YOU PAY CLOSER ATTENTION? THE CRIMES WERE REAL. THE ACTIONS, UNCONSCIONABLE. BUT DEAR READER, YOU DIDN'T KNOW. YOU WEREN'T INVOLVED. YOU'VE SIMPLY PURCHASED, OR BORROWED THE LATEST BEST SELLER AND FELL IN LOVE WITH PROSE.

THE JOLLY ROGER BLOG

THEFT OF ART, OF PEOPLE'S LIFE STORIES IS THE LOWEST OF LOW. YET, IT CONTINUES: RIP, RINSE, REPEAT. ALWAYS WITH A MANTRA TO READ, WRITE, REVIEW.

NOW, LET'S TRY A ONE-EIGHTY. WHAT IF ENOUGH WAS ENOUGH, AND THE DIRTY LAUNDRY WAS OVERDUE TO BE AIRED? WHAT IF THE SOURCE AUTHORS–THOSE WHOSE WORDS WERE RAPED AND CORRUPTED, ONE LINE AT A TIME, ONE PLOT, ONE CHARACTER. WHOSE LIFE BLOOD WAS USED TO CREATE DOZENS OF BEST SELLING WORKS. WHAT IF THEY ROSE UP AND TORE YOUR ROMANCELANDIA DOWN?

THOSE WORDS. THOSE CHARACTERS. THOSE LIVES WERE STOLEN—THEY WERE REAL.

BUT THERE REMAINS A MORALITY IN SOME OF US. WE
WON'T CROSS THE SAME LINE THEY DID. READERS
WANT ONE THING–ESCAPE. THEY CARE LITTLE FOR HOW
THOSE WORDS ARE ACHIEVED, ONLY THAT THEY'RE
AMAZING, HEART WRENCHING, LIFE CHANGING,
OBSESSIONS.
IF THE AUTHOR FEELS NO REMORSE, AND WHY WOULD
THEY? MONEY HAS BEEN MADE, AND NO ONE CAUGHT
ON TO THE SCAM. BESTSELLERS MADE BANK AND
PADDED THEIR NEXT PROJECT.
I THINK IF THE AUTHOR SHOWS NONE, NEITHER WILL
THEIR READERS. THEY PURELY WANT THE NEXT FIX.
ADDICTION IS A FUNNY THING.

THE JOLLY ROGER BLOG

AT SOME POINT YOU'D EXPECT TO QUERY THE SOURCE
PRODUCT, WOULDN'T YOU?
SO TELL ME, DEAR READER, WHAT IF IT WAS YOUR LIFE
STOLEN? WHAT WOULD YOU DO?
ME—MY LIFE WAS SACRIFICED, LIKE SO MANY OTHERS,
AND MY STORY WAS VAULTED.
OR WAS IT? IF YOU'RE READING THIS, I GUESS THEY
TOOK THEIR BUSINESS PLAN ONE STEP TOO FAR.

MUCH LOVE,
EVIE XOX

Evie began this little journey with warnings at every corner; well wishers were encouraged someone else would do what they couldn't. She sat quietly for the most part and behaved, edited everything to within an inch of its life, and held back. That's basic common sense and human decency. It's a shame most left theirs at the door on the climb to the top.

What would you sacrifice to reach the top?

Your life, your family?

What about your morality?

Sounds harsh, but that's what it takes to enter the game.

As the saying goes, rip, rinse, repeat—after all, it was there for the taking.

As Evie watched her story unfold, the same who were full of warnings, both legal and moral, rose higher. They had an end game which unfolded, not unexpectedly.

So, as a reader, thank you for opening this finale. Thank you for whatever reason you turned the first page. Oh, and I'm sorry, Kaye and Noel are still in there somewhere, it was never about them though as side characters.

I hope you didn't skim only to search for the fictional gossip. If you've been with us from the beginning with PuSh, you're aware of Kat's back story. Well, this little tie up connected a few more dots, and completes the circle, for now.

This isn't fanfic, or reworked public domain. This is how I was taught to write. Find a topic, research the hell out of it, and make sure it's your own, not some bastardized version of another person's work.

I guess this story never really ends, while the scammers continue to abuse loopholes. Will they be read, sure. Will they be remembered for the right reason, probably not.

Love or hate it, drop a review. It's what the numbers game is all about after all. Ask yourself, could any of it possibly be real? If you'd like to read how the story began, turn the page for a sample of PuSh, by Evie Campbell.

Acknowledgements

To the prima donnas who believe this is about them—I'd not waste my time. This is for the real talent out there, those whose words were pilfered and squandered by greed.

To the vague posters, did you think your threats weren't heard? You only made this easier to publish.

Sleep well in your ill gotten gains—a reckoning is coming.

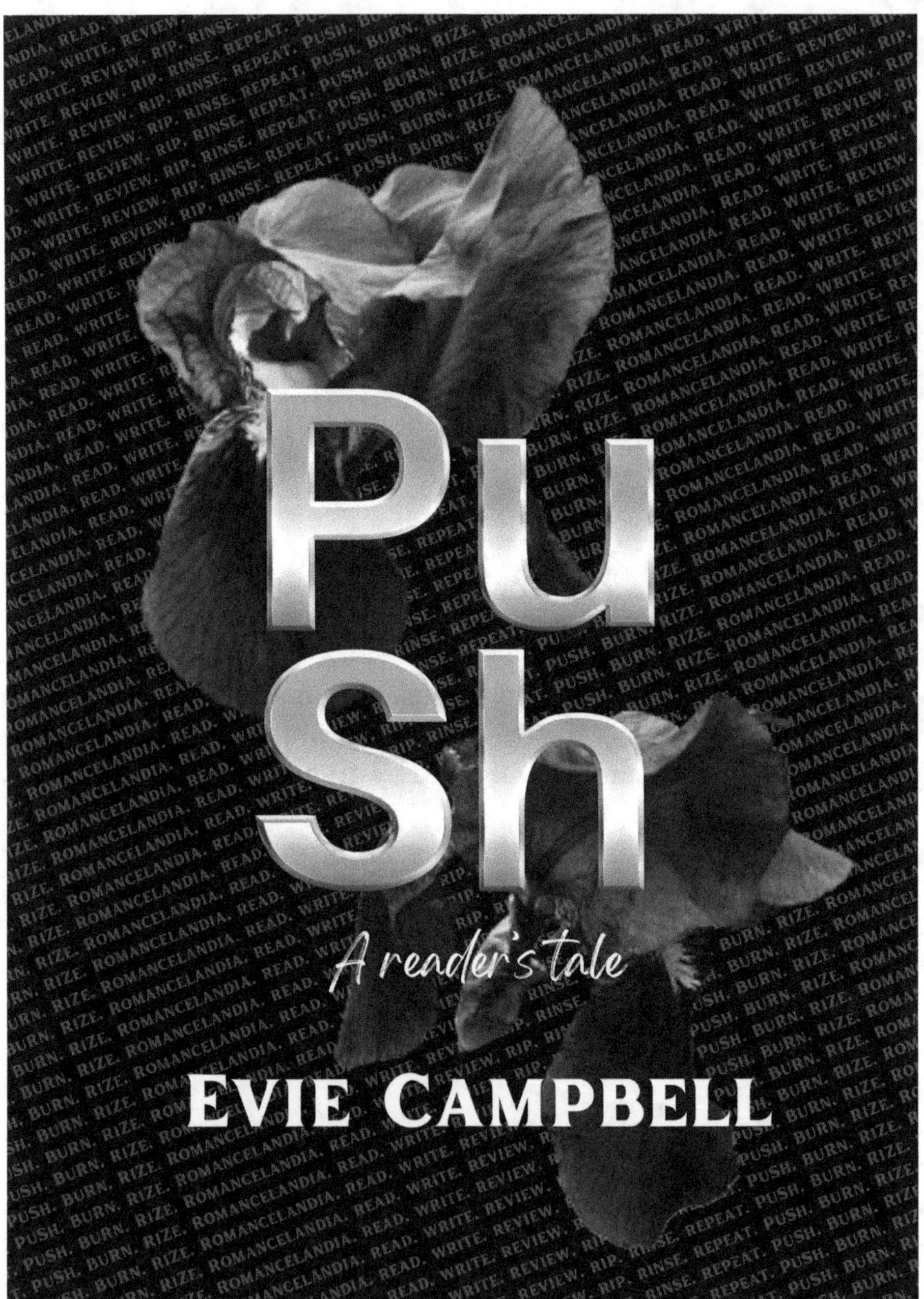

PuSh
A reader's tale
EVIE CAMPBELL

Kat - present.

11:35 a.m. Tuesday 2nd August.

"Kat? Are you home? Your gourmet meal's arrived." Sara's voice echoes from the empty atrium of my father's home. I hear the rustle of paper bags, as she moves into the kitchen with groceries.

Jotting down my last thoughts, keystrokes click on my typewriter-style keyboard, comforting me in their familiarity. I race to add another few random thoughts kicking around in my skull.

Readers remember the vermin, pure and simple. I'd liken them to roof rats, bastards are damn hard to get rid of. Cockroaches are a better analogy. They're able to survive a nuclear holocaust, determined little bastards. Bottom-feeding groups return with a vengeance, breeding the next mutant generation, unhindered.

"Sorry, I was on a roll. I had to get this down before it disappeared into the abyss." I chuckle at my joke. The dark depths of my hard drive consume thousands of words daily, never to see the light.

"You're going through with this then, Kat? You're finally going to publish?" Sara's excitement is almost contagious.

"Nope. It's for my benefit." If I could suppress the acrid taste in my mouth, contemplating going live, I'd take the risk.

Pursing her lips, an all too familiar scenario's about to play out. "What's the point then? It's written, what's the point if you keep polishing it? They're only going to return strengthened and immune to repercussions. Why leave them standing? How many more will suffer at their hands?"

"One, it's cathartic? Two, it's not my responsibility to sacrifice myself for others who are ignorant of the inner workings. Most people read for pure pleasure, they've no idea how indie functions. Why spoil it for someone else? Brutally shoving authors from pedestals, to show they're mere mortals achieves nothing. One day–one day I'll grow a set and take the plunge, not right now."

"And when you do? What's it going to resemble? A fluffy unicorn glitter fest, or hell and brimstone?"

My staunchest ally, Sara's always ready to rumble. If she hadn't picked me back up from the depths of a dark hole after Dale and the chat drama, I don't know where I'd be. "Napalm, hellfire, and big fucking boots—I'll throw it all at them. No one will see it coming and I'll sleep again at night."

"I'll bring the marshmallows and vodka for the bonfire, hon."

"It's a date, Sara."

"Don't leave it too long Kat. We love you. We want you back in the land of the living." Sara's reassurance warms my heart and adds to my resolve to make this right.

∞ ∞ ∞

Want more? You can find me and my alter ego by scanning the link below.

Books In This Series

Reprieve

* For readers 18+. If you enjoy a quick read, a sweet naive heroine, and a cinnamon roll hero, Dale and Belle's story may be for you.

Shattered & Broken

Mason

She strolled into my studio like she owned the place.

Well, she owned the building. My home. My sanctuary.

All bluff, and blunder, with no substance to her argument, "It's time for a renovation."

Hell, the place is almost new.

I see the broken woman behind her mask.

Lost. Alone. Searching.

I know her history and the world she inhabits, better than most.

Kat

You're only as old as the person you're, well you know what I mean.

I feel like a cougar, and I know, to never mix business with pleasure.

But I'm out of that market, and Mason's too young to be taken seriously.

I'll not shackle my baggage to him, nor hold him back. The mess I'm in–it's not one I'd drag anyone else into.

* For readers 18+. If you enjoy a quick read, a sweet naive heroine, and a cinnamon roll hero, Kat and Mason's story may be for you.

Bound & Disarray

Noel

Broken flowers are my specialty. I'm able to envision the beauty they hide, and encourage them to thrive and bloom.

This one's a keeper. Such a shame she doesn't understand her value outside of the boardroom.

Kaye

My work has been my life for as long as I can remember. I can't believe how quickly time passed me by. What do I have to offer a soul as old as Noel's with a mouth as dirty as a sailor's.

I don't understand what he sees in me, but the heat in the bedroom sets fire to the furnishings. Sometimes love finds you at the most inopportune moments.

* For readers 18+. If you enjoy a quick read, a sweet heroine, and a cheeky hero, Noel and Kaye's story may be for you.

Reprieve

Three book omnibus of the Reprieve short stories with extended content.